Daily Life in ANCIENT SUMER

Nick Hunter

a Capstone company — publishers for children

Raintree is an imprint of Capstone Global Library Limited, a company incorporated in England and Wales having its registered office at 7 Pilgrim Street, London, EC4V 6LB – Registered company number: 6695582

www.raintree.co.uk
myorders@raintree.co.uk

Text © Capstone Global Library Limited 2016
The moral rights of the proprietor have been asserted.

Edited by Linda Staniford and Holly Beaumont
Designed by Philippa Jenkins
Original illustrations © Capstone Global Library Limited 2015
Illustrated by Oxford Designers and Illustrators; caption characters and pages 42-43 by Philippa Jenkins
Picture research by Gina Kammer
Production by Victoria Fitzgerald
Originated by Capstone Global Library Ltd
Printed and bound in China by Leo Paper Products

ISBN 978 1 406 29852 9
19 18 17 16 15
10 9 8 7 6 5 4 3 2 1

British Library Cataloguing in Publication Data
A full catalogue record for this book is available from the British Library.

Acknowledgements
We would like to thank the following for permission to reproduce photographs: Art Resource, N.Y.: © Balage Balogh, 29; Bridgeman Images: Ancient Art and Architecture Collection Ltd./Impression of a cylinder seal depicting a marsh hunt with a reed boat, 3rd millennium BC (plaster), Sumerian, 23, Ashmolean Museum, University of Oxford, UK/ Tablet from Jamdat Nasr in Iraq, listing quantities of various commodities in archaic Sumerian (early cuneiform script) c.3200-3000 BC (clay), Sumerian, 37; Courtesy of the Penn Museum, image #B16665, 16; Getty Images: DEA /A. DE GREGORIO, 39, DEA PICTURE LIBRARY, 17, DEA/G. NIMATALLAH, 30, DEA/M. CARRIERI, 20, L. DE MASI, 43, Print Collector, 24, 38, Werner Forman, 18; Glow Images: Photographer name, 8; Mary Evans Picture Library: © Illustrated London News Ltd, 41; Newscom: akg-images, 6, KRT/RICH GLICKSTEIN, 7, Prisma, 27, 40, REUTERS/KIERAN DOHERTY, 32, Robert Harding/ Richard Ashworth, 10, Werner Forman/akg-images, 14, World History Archive, cover, 21, 25, ZUMAPRESS/Andrew Craft, 31; Science Source, 19, 35, Sheila Terry, 11; Shutterstock: Kamira, 5, Sergei25, 22, Vladimir Korostyshevskiy, 12.

Cover image: A detail from the Standard of Ur. This mosaic illustrates life in ancient Sumer and was discovered in the city of Ur in the 1920s.

We would like to thank Dr Mark Manuel for his help in the preparation of this book.

Every effort has been made to contact copyright holders of material reproduced in this book. Any omissions will be rectified in subsequent printings if notice is given to the publisher.

All the internet addresses (URLs) given in this book were valid at the time of going to press. However, due to the dynamic nature of the internet, some addresses may have changed, or sites may have changed or ceased to exist since publication. While the author and publisher regret any inconvenience this may cause readers, no responsibility for any such changes can be accepted by either the author or the publisher.

CONTENTS

Some words are shown in bold, **like this**. You can find out what they mean by looking in the glossary.

The first human **civilizations** developed between 5,000 and 6,000 years ago around the great rivers of Africa and Asia. People organized themselves into cities and states, often ruled by powerful kings. These people communicated with each other using written languages. They included the people of ancient Egypt, who lived along the River Nile, and the Indus Valley civilization of northern India. The ancient Sumerian civilization grew around the Rivers Tigris and Euphrates, in the area that is now Iraq.

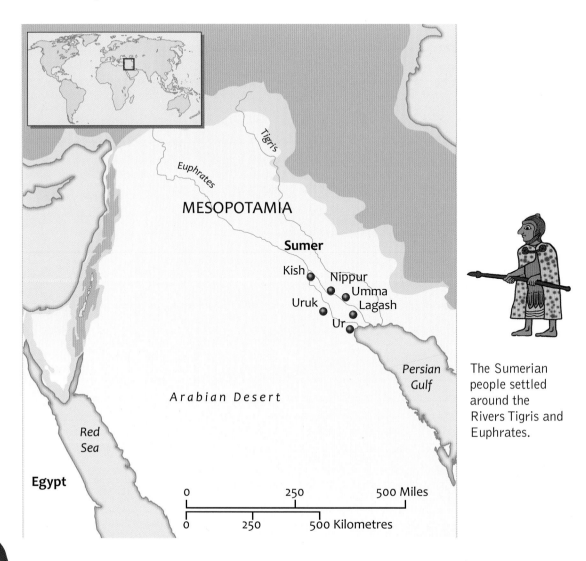

The Sumerian people settled around the Rivers Tigris and Euphrates.

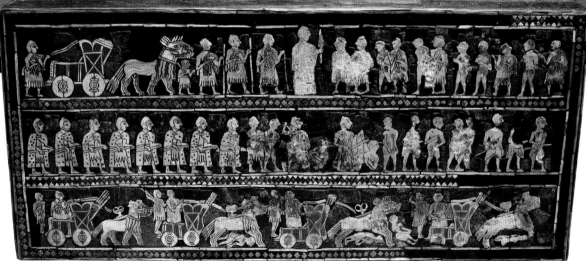

Culture of invention

The Sumerian civilization, which began around 3300 BC, was centred on several **city-states**, such as Kish and Ur. These were the first cities on Earth. The city was just one of many essential inventions created by the Sumerians, from the wheel to the way we divide the day into minutes and hours.

The Sumerian civilization came to an end around 2000 BC, when it was absorbed into neighbouring **cultures**. But the impact of the culture can still be felt almost 4,000 years later.

This object, called the Standard of Ur, was found in the tomb of a Sumerian queen. The mosaic pictures that cover it show how people lived more than 4,000 years ago.

HOW DO WE KNOW?

The Sumerian civilization ended approximately 4,000 years ago. We know more about its people and how they lived than about some more recent civilizations. This is because the Sumerians invented a form of writing, called **cuneiform** script. They did not write on paper, which would have decayed thousands of years ago, but on solid **tablets** of clay, which can be read by experts.

The first people settled in the region that became ancient Sumer in the centuries after 4500 BC. They farmed the land next to the two great rivers that flow through the region, draining the marshes around them. These people also introduced industries, such as weaving and metalworking.

First cities

People who spoke the Sumerian language came from further north in around 3300 BC. They began to build cities such as Uruk, which may be the world's oldest city. In the centuries that followed, there were at least 12 major cities founded. These cities included large public buildings, such as temples. They could only have been built by large groups of people working together.

Gudea was king of the Sumerian city of Lagash.

Culture and competition

The city-states were often in competition, especially for control of water supplies from the rivers. There were often disputes between cities, which were surrounded by walls to protect them from attack. However, many aspects of their culture were shared, such as their writing system and their talent for invention.

Floods can happen suddenly in the Euphrates and Tigris river valleys, especially when snows melt in the mountains from which the rivers flow.

THE GREAT FLOOD

Many Sumerian sources tell of a great flood that covered the land, probably around 3000 BC. This flood is mentioned in other cultures, including the sacred texts of Jewish and Christian religions. **Archaeologists** have found evidence of a major flood at this time. The rivers, which were so important to the Sumerians and their growing cities, also changed course at this time, leading to more disputes over access to water.

Communities in ancient Sumer ranged in size, from small villages to cities that were centres of power and religion. The largest cities, including Uruk, Ur and Kish, were probably home to around 50,000 people each.

HOW DO WE KNOW?

The earliest examples of writing were not poems or stories. They were accounts and records of who owned what. Written records were a way for rulers to control and count the people and goods in their states. These written records were created and read by officials called **scribes**.

City planning

Sumerian cities were not built to a particular plan. Homes and other buildings were regularly rebuilt, but the cities all contained similar types of building. The centre of the city included the main public buildings. Some of the biggest buildings were the temples of the main city gods, which may have also included living quarters and storehouses. Houses of rich and powerful families were probably close to these buildings. Beyond them lay the smaller mud-brick houses of ordinary people.

Homes and businesses of particular groups of people may have been grouped together. In one city, several buildings with baking ovens have been found in the same area. Cities included some very large houses, showing that some people were much richer than others.

Fresh air?

There were few public open spaces within the city. Public gatherings may have taken place outside the walls. There are no records of rubbish collection, so streets may have been full of rotting food and worse, providing rich pickings for stray dogs and pigs.

Some aspects of city layouts were not that different from the cities that are familiar to us today.

Supplying the city

Workshops created everything the city's people needed, from pots and clothes to metal tools and weapons. Large **granaries** and storehouses were needed to store the city's food. Cities were also filled with small temples and religious **shrines**.

Walled cities

The cities were surrounded by walls and fortifications. In Ur, one of the largest cities, the city centre was inside a defensive wall and another wall enclosed the rest of the settlement. The city also had two ports: one on the River Euphrates and another beside a **canal**. Walls could act as protection from floods as well as attacking armies.

This **ziggurat** is the only building that survives from the cities of Sumer.

THE FIRST WHEELS

The Sumerians were the first people to use wheels. Pictures of solid-wheeled carts have been found. These simple vehicles, pulled by oxen and donkeys, would only have been useful for short journeys. The same technology was also used to create potters' wheels.

Growing food

Beyond the city walls lay the farmland that was used to grow crops and raise animals to feed the people. This included garden areas for growing fruit and vegetables. Fields for other crops had to be **irrigated** by canals that circulated water from the rivers. Beyond this area was the dry scrubland where farm animals grazed. The annual harvest was the key to city life; without it the people would starve.

Transport

Although some cities had roads, most goods and people were transported between the city-states by boat. Goods could be loaded and unloaded at **wharves** on the major rivers, or on canals joined to them. All cities were built close to waterways for transport, and so that water could be channelled to the fields to irrigate crops.

Divisions in society

When the first cities were founded, the people of Sumer probably ruled themselves. These were small communities, and together they made decisions, although some people had more influence because of wealth or a strong personality. But a growing population and more complex cities soon required a single person to take key decisions.

These temporary governors eventually became powerful kings of the city-states. Power was usually passed on to the king's younger brother or his eldest son when he died. Rulers didn't always have things their own way. They may have been advised by councils of leading citizens, and they couldn't afford to upset the powerful priests.

This is the carved head of an Akkadian king, who may have been King Sargon.

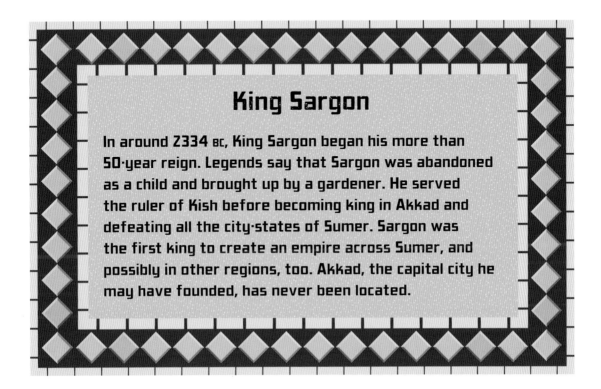

King Sargon

In around 2334 BC, King Sargon began his more than 50-year reign. Legends say that Sargon was abandoned as a child and brought up by a gardener. He served the ruler of Kish before becoming king in Akkad and defeating all the city-states of Sumer. Sargon was the first king to create an empire across Sumer, and possibly in other regions, too. Akkad, the capital city he may have founded, has never been located.

A good king?

Kings liked to celebrate their victories over their rivals, but some seem to have looked after their people, too. King Uru-inim-gina of Lagash claimed that royal officials were taking goods unfairly from the people and the temples. He removed the **corrupt** officials and introduced a fairer system to protect the poor. We don't know whether ordinary people agreed with him about his achievements, but Uru-inim-gina was eventually driven from power when he lost a battle with Lagash's fierce rival, Umma.

How was society organized?

The king of a city-state was the servant of the local god. If he displeased the god then the people were at risk. As well as these religious duties, he also had to manage the city. This included arranging and paying for the public building works and irrigation canals. Many of the people within each city-state would have worked directly for the king or the temple, and would be paid in food.

This detail from the Standard of Ur shows a banquet scene. The largest seated figure is the king.

Below the king and priests in Sumerian society were other leading families who controlled their own land and employed others. Most families either owned their own land, worked as craftspeople and traders, or worked for the temple or palace. At the bottom of society were **slaves**, although Sumerian cities didn't rely on large numbers of slaves to do the work.

Powerful women

Women had more influence than in some other parts of the ancient world. Although women did not usually become rulers, they could be in charge of large **estates** for the king, and could own property. Women could also hold some of the key jobs in ancient Sumer, such as scribe or priestess.

Law and order

Sumerian rulers also developed laws to manage their states. The Code of Ur-Nammu is a list of laws set down in around 2050 BC by a king of Ur. It covers topics such as treatment of slaves, divorce and disputes over farming and water.

SOCIAL CLIMBING

People could rise through the Sumerian class system. The only female ruler on the Sumerian king lists was called Ku-Bau, and she started off as a tavern keeper.

When the Sumerian city-states were founded, they each worshipped their own god. The main temples to these gods were built in the heart of the new cities, and the priests who governed the temples held great power and influence. Kings later became the rulers of the city, but religion and its priests retained a strong hold on Sumerian life.

This disc shows Enheduanna and servants, including her personal scribe.

Enheduanna

Enheduanna was a remarkable woman. Not only was she the high priestess of Ur, but the poems and hymns she wrote make her history's very first named writer. Enheduanna had a head start in life as the daughter of King Sargon, but she was obviously a strong woman herself. King Sargon faced many enemies in the city-states he had conquered, and Enheduanna fought off attempts to force her from her post.

The gods

Over the centuries, different city-states began to worship the same group of gods, although individual gods often kept their special place in the religion of one city. Enlil was the creator god, who had separated Heaven and Earth. Other gods looked after things that were important to the Sumerians: Enki was god of fresh water in rivers and marshes, so important for farming in the dry landscape. People believed that the gods met in the city of Nippur. Other city-states helped to build and maintain the temples of this holy city, where the gods would make important decisions affecting the people. This included deciding which Sumerian city would hold power over the others.

As Sumerian wealth grew, more impressive temples were built, including dramatic ziggurats, which probably had a shrine at the top.

Religion and Life

Religion was very personal to the Sumerians. Individuals and communities had to honour the gods and give them presents to avoid disasters. Cities were full of temples and small shrines to various gods.

The Sumerians believed there were many ways to offend the gods. Written tablets list around 200 sins. These included causing trouble for your family or killing an animal without reason.

Working at the temple

It was the priest's job to serve the statue or image of the god. This included giving them food and clothes. The temple was seen as the home of the city's god. Temples were often large complexes with many rooms, including kitchens to cook food for the gods and the priests who lived within its walls. Temple workers included scribes, musicians and servants, as well as the priests themselves.

Statues like this were often found in temples. They were probably left by people who came to pray for some kind of favour from the god.

Death and the afterlife

The Sumerians believed that, after death, people would travel to the **Underworld**. Writings described this as a dark and unpleasant place. Archaeologists have found graveyards containing hundreds of tombs, which help them to understand much more about how the Sumerians lived and died.

Archaeologist Leonard Woolley discovered many Sumerian grave goods during excavations at Ur.

GRAVE GOODS

When people died, their graves were filled with food, tools, games or musical instruments. These were probably things the dead Sumerian would need in the Underworld. The more luxurious goods in royal graves may have been gifts for the lords of the Underworld. The poorer people probably had no goods to be buried with them.

The city-states of Sumer were constantly in competition with each other. Different states gained power over the others at different times after 3000 BC, before the Akkadian King Sargon extended his power over the whole region after 2200 BC. Sargon and his successors had to fight many rebellions to keep control.

Weapons and armour

Sumerian troops fought with metal weapons, including swords, daggers, spears and arrows. Stone **maces** were also popular. Metal helmets and shields protected shoulders, while long leather cloaks covered with metal discs acted as armour.

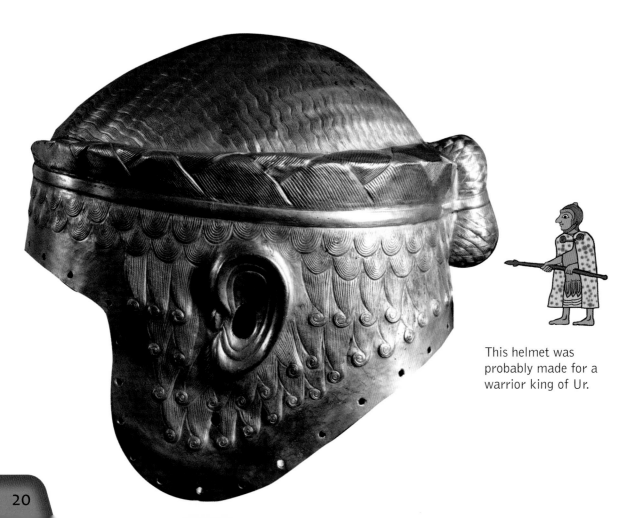

This helmet was probably made for a warrior king of Ur.

The Standard of Ur shows a victorious king of Ur around 2500 BC. Alongside the chariots and soldiers of his army are captured prisoners. These prisoners probably faced slavery or even death. On a stone carving celebrating a victory for Lagash over its rival Umma, prisoners are shown being carried in a net.

Sumerian military technology included war chariots.

CITY-STATES AT WAR

In about 2400 BC, a bitter argument began between the city-states of Umma and Lagash about their borders and control of water supplies. The dispute rumbled on for many years between the rulers of these states, sometimes erupting in conflict. Eventually it was settled by the ruler of another state, Kish. This is one of the earliest political disputes ever recorded, and it seems that the powerful ruler of Kish had some power over the kings of these smaller states.

Wars were fought over the boundaries between city-states because this was land that really mattered to the rulers. Kings believed that their power came from their gods, but if people didn't have enough to eat, the rulers would soon be in trouble. Most Sumerian people worked on growing and producing food.

Date palms grew well in the hot, dry climate of Sumer.

Fruit and vegetables

Dates were the main fruit grown in the gardens close to the city and alongside the river and canals. They could be eaten or their juice could be used to sweeten other foods and make wine. The leaves of the date palms provided shade for other fruit plants, such as pomegranates, figs and apples. The gardeners also grew vegetables such as onions.

Fishermen used small boats to catch fish in the great rivers or hunt in the marshes of Sumer.

The farming year

In the autumn, gangs of men worked to irrigate the fields in time to plant wheat and barley. Water was essential to make the ground soft enough for ploughs pulled by oxen and donkeys, to break it up. The crop had to be regularly watered before it was harvested in the spring. Farmers used **scythes** made of **flint** or copper to harvest the crop. Other crops, such as sesame, which provided oil, were grown in summer.

HOW DO WE KNOW?

Labourers with no land of their own worked for the temple or the palace, which owned much of the farmland. Clay tablets were used to record the amount of food labourers received in exchange for their work.

From the farm to the table

Wealthy Sumerians probably had quite a varied diet, as they would have had the pick of the wide range of crops grown in the gardens and fields. However, the main foods would have been flat bread, fish, dates and vegetables. This diet was quite healthy, and low in sugar.

They would also have the option of eating meat, including pigs, sheep and goats, which grazed on the rough scrubland beyond the wheat and barley fields. Animals were also hunted for their meat, ranging from deer and gazelles to hares and birds. Military victories were celebrated with lavish feasts for the king and his close friends, but ordinary people would have little chance of feasting.

This early writing tablet is a record of the allocation of barley rations to workers.

Ordinary farmers were able to grow fruit and vegetables for themselves and may have even owned some animals. However, the poorest labourers who worked for the temple or the king had to take whatever rations they were given, usually barley, beer, dates and fish.

Textile crops

Crops were also needed to make clothes. A record from Ur records a flock of 350,000 sheep. Sheep's wool and animal skins were used for textiles and clothes. Flax was also grown to make lightweight linen.

The Standard of Ur shows some of the animals that the Sumerians farmed.

BREWING BEER

Sumerians may have been the first people to brew beer. This drink, made from barley, was certainly an essential part of their diet. Beer was thick, like porridge, and was probably drunk through a straw, which would filter out some of the lumps.

Before the first cities developed, most people were farmers or hunters, growing or catching enough food for themselves and their families. As farming methods improved, not everyone was needed to work on the land. People could now do other jobs, using their skills to make tools or work for the government.

Top jobs included working as priests or scribes. Scribes were very skilled and highly trained people, and this gave them a lot of power in the Sumerian city. As the only people who could read and write, they were responsible for recording and managing all aspects of city life. Scribes wrote on clay tablets using a tool called a stylus to make marks in the wet clay.

HOW DO WE KNOW?

Clay writing tablets are very long-lasting. There are around 130,000 writing tablets from ancient Mesopotamia stored in the British Museum alone.

Becoming a scribe

New scribes were often the sons, and occasionally daughters, of scribes, so they already came from educated and wealthy families. It took years of training to become a scribe, but the rewards were great.

MEASURING TIME

Sumerian scribes developed our idea of time. By 2400 BC, they had developed the idea of a year that included the whole farming cycle from one planting to the next. The Sumerians were also the first people to divide the day into 24 units (hours). Their number system was based on units of 60, which is still used in units of time, such as minutes and seconds.

This statue shows the man in charge of building work near the city of Uruk in about 2300 BC.

Merchants and traders

Many of the beautiful things found in the graves of wealthy Sumerians tell us about more than the people who owned them. They include materials that must have been brought to Sumer from as far away as India, by traders and merchants.

Trade routes

The Sumerians imported precious lapis lazuli from Afghanistan; other precious stones came from India. Gold and silver may have come from elsewhere on the Persian Gulf coast. It wasn't just luxury goods that were imported: copper from Arabia was needed for all kinds of tools.

The Rivers Tigris and Euphrates were the trade routes of their day. Traders could travel north to the region that is now Syria and Turkey, or south into the Indian Ocean. At first these traders may have been sent by the palace or temple authorities, but they later became rich merchants in their own right. In return for the luxury goods, they probably traded food and crafts, such as fine pottery and textiles from Sumer.

MONEY

The Sumerians didn't use money. Craftspeople were paid for their work in essential products, such as barley, or even by use of a piece of land, usually provided by the temple or the royal palace. Individuals would value goods or services in exchange for a common material. For example, a new tool or weapon could be worth a certain amount of copper. There were written lists of fair prices for different goods.

Trading voyages were long and dangerous. Traders made offerings of boats at the temple to ensure a safe journey.

Building projects involved moving large blocks of stone with very limited technology.

Craftspeople and the working class

Simple goods, such as cooking pots or farming tools, were probably made in small workshops or at home. Skilled craftspeople created high-quality pottery, metal goods and textiles for temple use and trade. Women and girls worked in large workshops weaving textiles in lots of different styles. Pottery was created using potter's wheels.

City authorities controlled metalworking workshops. All metal had to be brought to Sumer from elsewhere, but Sumerian craftspeople created a wide range of weapons, tools and containers using copper and tin. Gold and silver were used to make jewellery.

Only the most skilled craftspeople would have been allowed to make the beautiful luxury goods found in royal graves. They would pass their skills and knowledge on to their children, and others, in a system of **apprenticeships.**

Kings and temples used slaves as part of their workforce. They were often prisoners of war but could also be people from the city who had committed a crime or fallen on hard times. Parents might even sell their children into slavery if they were in desperate need or couldn't pay a debt. In this case, slavery might just be for a short period, and people could buy back their freedom.

Building the city

Sumerian workers built some of the most impressive palaces, temples and ziggurats of the ancient world. City workers included specialist builders and brickmakers, but a large workforce would be needed to build these monumental structures. These probably included the army and slaves, but ordinary Sumerians had to help out too.

The Great Ziggurat of Ur still towers over the desert in southern Iraq.

Sumerian houses were usually built from mud-bricks, made from a mixture of mud and straw. These bricks were used for town walls and public buildings, as well as homes. Homes for poorer people included huts made from reeds or tents.

Houses were usually built with rooms opening on to a central courtyard. Privacy was obviously important as rooms looked inwards to the courtyard, rather than having windows on the outer walls. Windows and doors were small, to keep the rooms cool in summer and warm in winter. Flat roofs could be used as extra living space.

WATERPROOFING

Sumerians were some of the first people to use oil. Thick oil, called bitumen, wells up to the surface in this region. The Sumerians used it to waterproof their buildings.

HOW DO WE KNOW?

Mud bricks were a handy building material as they were cheap and readily available. Unfortunately, we don't know much about what homes looked like because the bricks don't survive being buried for thousands of years. However, archaeologists can still study the stone foundations of many buildings.

Home comforts

Ordinary houses probably had very little furniture, but the houses of the rich were a bit more luxurious. Carvings show the rich sitting on chairs and thrones, alongside tables. Palaces had bathing rooms and even toilets, with raised brick seats above a pit or drain.

Food was kept cool in large pottery jars and containers.

Family Life

Family connections were an essential part of Sumerian life. Land for farming was usually held by the whole extended family, and could only be sold with everyone's agreement. If some natural disaster, such as a flood, destroyed a family's crop, the extended family would have to help each other out with food in order to survive.

Marriage and children

A couple's parents would arrange their marriage, which was often sealed with a contract inscribed on a clay tablet. The husband and father was the undisputed leader of the family for as long as he lived, although women were allowed to own property. Husbands could divorce their wives if the couple had no children, and children were expected to obey their father completely. A legal code from later Mesopotamian civilization warns that "if a son strikes his father, they shall cut off his hand". Many Sumerian songs and proverbs describe the close bonds of love and respect between members of the family, especially between fathers and sons.

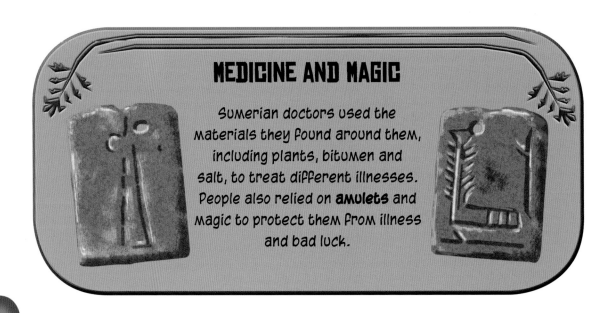

MEDICINE AND MAGIC

Sumerian doctors used the materials they found around them, including plants, bitumen and salt, to treat different illnesses. People also relied on **amulets** and magic to protect them from illness and bad luck.

Country Life

Not everyone lived outside cities. In villages away from the city, several households of related families might be grouped together, along with workshops and storehouses.

Utnapishtim, shown here with his wife, was a legendary figure who built a giant boat at the time of the great flood, to rescue his family and their animals.

Growing up

Families normally had between two and four children who lived to be adults, although many people died during childhood. It was important to have a male child to inherit the family's land, and children were sometimes adopted. Children lived in the family household until they were married.

As in other ancient civilizations, most children didn't go to school. Even kings and nobles would probably not be able to read and write. Children helped in the fields or in the workshops as soon as they were old enough, or looked after younger brothers and sisters while their parents worked. They probably also helped out with chores around the home, such as fetching water from the public well.

For most children, toys would have been simple or homemade. Royal tombs contain fine board games and musical instruments. Ordinary families may have had simpler versions of these.

HOW DO WE KNOW?

We know what scribes learned from the tablets they used at school. Some were like dictionaries, listing the symbols for gods, animals and other useful words. Archaeologists have even been able to study the tablets written by student scribes to see how their skills developed.

Scribal schools

School was for the lucky few, mostly boys, who were training to be scribes. Experienced scribes taught them maths and classic stories from Sumerian history, as well as how to create cuneiform writing. Some scribes probably learned to be architects for city buildings.

Many of the tablets created by scribes were accounts or lists of different goods.

Weaving textiles to make clothing was a major industry in ancient Sumer. There were many different styles of cloth available and people obviously cared about how they looked, especially the rich.

Fashions of the rich

Wool was the main material used to make clothes. Noble women wore long-sleeved jackets, which would have been adorned with metal rings, beads and shells to brighten them up, and possibly to fasten them as well. Sumerian art shows women wearing long robes. The most striking part of a noble woman's dress would have been a magnificent decorated headdress, made of cloth or felt.

This jewellery was found at the Royal Cemetery at Ur.

Men wore a garment a bit like a shirt and jacket, with a headcloth tied with a string of beads. Sumerian art often shows men in long skirts made of shaggy material, with their heads shaved. This may have been normal dress for religious ceremonies or formal occasions. Sharp blades were used for shaving the chin or the head, although some men are also shown with beards. Both men and women used brightly coloured make-up.

HOW DO WE KNOW?

Much of what we know about Sumerian clothing and jewellery comes from the graveyard at Ur, discovered by Leonard Woolley in 1922. It housed 16 stone tombs, which contained the bodies, belongings and traces of clothing belonging to powerful citizens.

Rich Sumerians wore jewellery made with precious materials from outside Sumer, including gold and lapis lazuli.

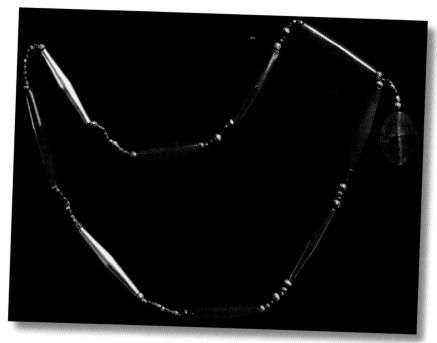

Everyday clothes

We know much less about ordinary people's clothes. Small figures left at temples show women in woollen or linen dresses. These may have been coloured or decorated with beads. Those who worked in the fields would have worn lightweight clothes to protect them from the hot sun.

Religious festivals during the year gave most Sumerians a rare chance to enjoy themselves. The most important festival was New Year, which was a time for feasts and celebrations.

Popular sports included wrestling and boxing. The Sumerians may also have played a version of polo. Instead of riding horses, they played the game sitting on the shoulders of other men. Board games were a more relaxed way of passing the time, and several such games have been discovered in the graves of noble Sumerians. These games used dice that were not too different from the ones we use today.

The Royal Game of Ur is a race game for two players. It was made at least 4,400 years ago.

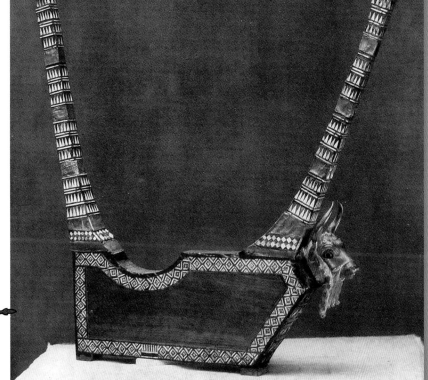

Musical instruments were often decorated with fine materials, but ordinary Sumerians probably played much simpler homemade versions.

Music and dance

The Sumerians loved music. They played stringed instruments like lyres and harps or pipes made from reed and metal, accompanied by drums and cymbals. We'll never know what the music sounded like, but we know that people composed songs and danced.

Written and spoken words

Most Sumerian writing was to do with everyday life and accounts. But scribes also recorded stories, poems and songs that were part of their culture. Most people wouldn't have known these written versions, as they couldn't read, but they were passed from one generation to the next by being retold and sung at festivals and family gatherings. There were probably many other stories and songs that were never written down. This reminds us that, however much we know of the amazing world of ancient Sumer, there is always more to find out.

A day in the life of a Sumerian boy

My name is Hulla. I live in the great city of Ur. When I go to the wharf, I hear the traders talk about the amazing places they've been. I'd love to do the same one day but, for now, this is the best place in the world to live.

I wake up every day to the sounds of the city, like the trundling carts and the dogs fighting over the rubbish in the streets. As soon as the sun comes up, my mother shouts for me to get the water so my father can get ready to go to the fields. My mother and sister work in the weaving workshop at the temple. My aunty and grandmother also live with us, so the house is always busy while we're eating our breakfast beer. Mum says it's the most important meal of the day. Normally, I help out in the fields. There's always something to do: planting seeds, watering, or cleaning out the canals after the flood.

If I can, I slip away to meet my friend Namkuzu. He goes to scribal school and I love finding out everything he's learning. He's always complaining about the hard work and tough discipline, but he doesn't know how lucky he is. I'm trying to learn how to write the names of different animals. I always honour the gods and hope that one day, I might be able to be a junior scribe. Otherwise, I'll be spending my life working in the burning sun just like everyone else I know.

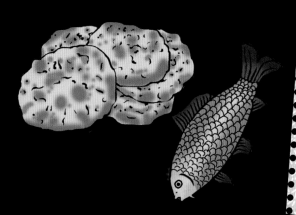

Mum got paid today, with fresh bread, fish and beans from the temple. I played everyone some tunes on my reed pipe after dinner. They all really enjoyed it, and said I should spend more time practising.

If you want to get on in life, you have to please the gods and carry a lucky amulet like this one.

AROUND 6000 BC
Village settlements begin in Mesopotamia

3300 BC
Founding of first Sumerian city-states and first use of cuneiform writing on tablets; Uruk is largest city in Sumer at this time

2900 BC
Beginning of Early Dynastic Period, during which Sumerian city-states battle each other for control of water and land

2800 BC
Etana, ruler of Kish, unites the city-states under his leadership

2600 BC
The start of the period when the Royal Cemetery at Ur is used to bury rulers and leading citizens of Ur

2500 BC
Conflict between Lagash and Umma over boundaries; the dispute continues for many generations

2400 BC
Uru-inim-gina is ruler of Lagash and introduces reforms to protect his people from corrupt officials

2334 BC
King Sargon's reign begins in Akkad. Sargon was probably the first king to rule all of ancient Sumer. Sumer's daughter, Enheduanna, becomes high priestess of Ur and the world's first named author.

2250 BC
King Naram-Sin, Sargon's grandson, declares himself King of the Four Quarters of the World and reduces the other kings of Sumer to the status of governors

2100 BC
King Ur-Nammu of Ur becomes overall king of Sumer, the first king of what has been called the Third Dynasty of Ur

2000 BC
End of distinct Sumerian civilization as their culture merges with neighbouring civilizations

1853
First excavation of the Great Ziggurat of Ur by British consul J.E. Taylor

1857
Confirmation that archaeologists have finally deciphered cuneiform writing when four scholars independently and correctly translate a Mesopotamian tablet

1922
Team of archaeologists led by Leonard Woolley begins detailed excavation of Ur, including around 1,800 graves in the so-called Royal Cemetery

amulet good-luck charm, like a locket, usually worn around the neck

apprenticeship when a young person works with an expert in a craft or job to learn their trade

archaeologist person who studies the bones, tools and other objects of ancient people to learn about past human life and activities

canal waterway created by people for transport or to carry water to fields

city-state state made up of a city and the land that surrounds it

civilization way of life of a particular place or group of people at a particular time

corrupt acting dishonestly or wrongly in return for money or power

culture customs and beliefs that are shared by a group of people, including religion, art and language

cuneiform wedge-shaped writing used in ancient Sumer

estate farmland owned by a rich landowner or organization

flint hard grey stone that can be sharpened to make tools

granary building used to store grain and other harvested crops

irrigate use canals (or ditches) to carry water from a river or lake to crops in fields

mace heavy club, usually with a spiked or metal head

scribe person who could read and write, who often served as a high official

scythe hand-held cutting tool used to harvest crops

shrine small temple or holy place where worshippers honour a god

slave person who is not free and has to work for an owner for no payment

tablet piece of clay or stone with writing or markings on it

Underworld place where the Sumerians believed the spirits of the dead went

wharf (plural: wharves) level structure built out into a harbour to which ships or other vessels can be moored to load and unload goods

ziggurat monumental temple tower, with each layer smaller than the one below it

Books

Ancient Iraq (Eyewitness), Philip Steele (Dorling Kindersley, 2007)
Ancient Sumer (Great Civilisations), Tracey Kelly (Franklin Watts, 2014)
Ancient Sumer (The History Detective Investigates), Kelly Davis (Wayland, 2014)
Tomb Explorers (Treasure Hunters), Nicola Barber (Raintree, 2013)

Websites

www.britishmuseum.org/explore/cultures/middle_east/sumerians.aspx
The British Museum website takes a detailed look at several objects that help us to understand ancient Sumer.

www.khanacademy.org/humanities/history/ancient-medieval/Ancient/v/standard-of-ur--c--2600-2400-b-c-e
This video explores the Standard of Ur, one of the most amazing finds from ancient Sumer.

www.penn.museum/games/cuneiform.shtml
Learn more about cuneiform writing from Penn Museum, Philadelphia, USA.

www.penn.museum/sites/iraq/?page_id=28
This website includes details about the amazing tomb of Queen Pu-abi, and a short video showing how her headdress was reconstructed.

Places to visit

Unfortunately, it's not possible for most people to visit the sites of the Sumerian city-states, partly because of distance but also because this region has suffered disastrous wars in recent years. Sumerian civilization did not leave many ruins that are visible today, apart from the Great Ziggurat at Ur. However, many of the treasures of ancient Sumer can be found in this museum:

British Museum
Great Russell Street
London
WC1B 3DG
www.britishmuseum.org